Releasing the Mantle of Prayer

Dr. Elise Banks

Releasing the Mantle of Prayer

Copyright © 2015 by Dr. Elise Banks

All Rights Reserved. No part of this publication may be reproduced, stored in a retrieval system, or transmitted, in any form or in any means – by electronic, mechanical, photocopying, recording, or otherwise – without prior written permission.

Unless otherwise noted all scripture quotations are taken from King James Version. Scripture quotations are taken from the Holy Bible, King James Version (Public Domain).

GOD'S WORD Translation (GW)

GOD'S WORD is a copyrighted work of God's Word to the Nations. Scripture Quotations marked "God's Word" are used by permission. Copyright 1995 by God's Word to the Nations. Used by permission of Baker Publishing Group. All rights reserved.

New American Standard Bible (NASB)
Scripture quotations marked "NASB" are taken from the New American Standard Bible®, Copyright © 1960, 1962, 1963, 1968, 1971, 1972, 1973, 1975, 1977, 1995 by The Lockman Foundation. Used by permission.

New International Version (NIV)
Scripture quotations marked (NIV) are taken from the Holy Bible, New International Version®, NIV®.

Copyright © 1973, 1978, 1984 by Biblica, Inc.™ Used by permission of Zondervan. All rights reserved worldwide.

New King James Version (NKJV)
Scripture quotations marked "NKJV" are taken from the New King James Version. Copyright © 1982 by Thomas Nelson, Inc. Used by permission. All rights reserved.

Bible text from the New King James Version® is not to be reproduced in copies or otherwise by any means except as permitted in writing by Thomas Nelson, Inc.,

Attn: Bible Rights and Permissions, P.O. Box 141000, Nashville, TN 37214-1000.

New Revised Standard Version (NRSV)
Scripture quotations marked "NRSV" are taken from the New Revised Standard Version Bible, copyright 1989, Division of Christian Education of the National Council of the Churches of Christ in the United States of America. Used by permission. All rights reserved.

Rotherham Emphasized Bible (Rotherham)
The Bible text designated Rotherham is from The Emphasized Bible by J.B. Rotherham, originally published by Samuel Bagster and Sons in 1902. The electronic text is by Larry Nelson, Box 2083, Rialto, CA 92376. (www.stepbible.org/version.jsp?version=Rotherham)

Requests for permission to make copies of this work should be sent to:

Restored Ministries International
P. O. Box 886
Lindenhurst, NY 11757

ISBN 10: 151725096X
ISBN 13: 978-1517250966
Printed in the United States of America

Cover Design & Layout by D'edge Media, LLC / dedgemedia.com

DEDICATION

To my special gifts

My daughters, Doria and Keesha, and my grandson, Kamron. I love you so much! You walked with me through the fires of testing and adversities and years of severe loss. You have been there as I persevered to receive this mantle of prayer. Thank you for your love and support even when you didn't fully understand the call, mission, and the mandate on my life. You have blessed me beyond measure.

I'm so thankful for and proud of you.

ACKNOWLEDGEMENTS

To my Apostolic Father and Spiritual Covering, Archbishop Alfred A. Owens, Jr. Thank you for loving and accepting me before I became fruit. You have covered, nurtured, and protected the seed of me and who I am to become. Your generous spirit and unconditional love truly makes you a leader after God's own heart. I am honored to walk in your shadow.

Ronalda Sedeno, Project Coordinator. Thank you for your push, for the many hours you labored and watched over this assignment. Your patience, expertise, and support is greatly appreciated. May God reward and richly bless you.

Cassandra Johnson, My Abishai. Thank you for coming to find me. You are the answer to unspoken prayer and the wind beneath my wings. Your heart for ministry and love for me has been deeply expressed in your service and covering. Only God can reward and repay you for being such a tremendous blessing to me. I'm eternally grateful for the gift of you.

Reverend Barbara Metz and Pastor Novella Harris. Thank you for your impartation of prayer and our many years of praying together – "The Circle Shall Never Be Broken!"

Lastly,

To the unsung heroes of faith – All the intercessors and prayer warriors, especially those of The Recovery Zone Prayer Encounter. I am so honored and blessed to serve as your spiritual midwife every week. You have helped me fulfill my destiny and walk in the shoes of a praying woman. Thank you for trusting and joining me at the altar of prayer. Don't stop praying – There is Power in Prayer!

CONTENTS

Foreword 1

Introduction 3

CHAPTER 1: Spiritual Understanding of a Mantle 6

CHAPTER 2: The Mantle of Prayer 11

CHAPTER 3: Touching the Mantle 17

CHAPTER 4: Releasing the Mantle 22

CHAPTER 5: Prayer to Release the Mantle of Favor 26

CHAPTER 6: Prayer to Release the Mantle of Healing and Divine Health 30

CHAPTER 7: Prayer to Release the Mantle of Prosperity and Financial Release 35

CHAPTER 8: Prayer to Release the Mantle of Restoration and Blessing 39

CHAPTER 9: Prayer to Release the Mantle of Glory 44

CHAPTER 10: The Power of Prayer 49

CHAPTER 11: An Encounter with Glory 59

About the Author 61

FOREWORD

I give God honor and glory for His chosen, powerful, Apostolic-Prophetic Prayer Warrior in this season, Apostle Dr. Elise Banks. I have found her to be a vessel of honor unto the Lord appointed to help release a Mantle of Prayer over the people of God to help shift them into their divine season of

1. Uncommon Favor;
2. The Glory of God;
3. Supernatural Healing and Divine Health;
4. Prosperity and Increase; and
5. Total and Complete Restoration.

Dr. Banks is a no hold back, pulling down strongholds Intercessor and gift to the Body of Christ at-large with her weekly National Prayer Encounters. If you have yet to experience The Recovery Zone Prayer Encounter Line, then the next best experience would be to read this book. With each page, you will be greatly inspired and encouraged by the force of prayer and your spirit will be activated. With the supernatural authority delegated by Jesus Christ and empowered by the Holy Spirit, the Woman of God leads you into your set time of favor; releases the manifestation of God's presence and power; revives your soul; pulls down and casts out spirits of infirmity and every manner of sickness and disease. Through the power of God, Apostle Banks, activates the spirit of prosperity and increase; and ultimately, brings you into a dynamic, culminating, high place of total and complete restoration! A place where everything is in divine order and alignment according to God's word, will, and way.

Apostle Elise Banks is a profound Prayer Leader and Warrior for the End Times. God's favor goes before her, therefore, she is more than able to lead the people of God into their harvest in the Due Season. I encourage those who are seeking a fresh anointing and impartation to get in a quiet zone and get ready to be strengthened and activated to arise in the fullness of the Mantle of Prayer. Prepare to gain access to unusual favor, healing, blessings, miracles, power, overflow, and abundance.

To God be all the glory......

Apostle Lougenia TrailBlazer Rucker
Divine Diamonds Ministries

INTRODUCTION

Releasing the Mantle of Prayer, will usher you into the divine presence and a personal audience with God. Position yourself to be refreshed, renewed, revived, and empowered in the presence of the Most High God. Prepare to see your family, community, and personal life changed in accordance with the will and purpose of God. As these Prayer Mantles are released upon you, your life will be forever changed as you are transformed through the divine power of prayer.

I encourage you to not just read this book, but truly pray through the prayers and establish them as your own. Decree and declare these prayers over your life and establish them as a part of your divine inheritance. Consider the words of prayer within these covers as a guidepost to the answers God has established since the beginning of time.

These five prayer targets reflect the prayer requests I receive most often from people. I believe that your faith will be activated through these supplications – *Prayer to Release the Mantle of Favor, Prayer to Release the Mantle of Healing and Divine Health, Prayer to Release the Mantle of Prosperity and Financial Release, Prayer to Release the Mantle of Restoration and Blessing, and Prayer to Release the Mantle of Glory.* In addition, they are petitions that I have personally prayed unto God. I pray that as you walk through these prayer points you will see breakthrough, turnaround, and supernatural miracles of God's goodness in your life.

Rejoice as you receive a divine impartation that will release a mantle of Spiritual Power and fresh anointing of glory upon your life.

Chapter 1

Spiritual Understanding of a Mantle

A mantle is a garment of distinction. Webster's Dictionary defines a mantle as a figurative cloak symbolizing preeminence or authority; something that covers, enfolds, or envelops. A mantle is an emblem of authority and symbol of spiritual covering. There were two styles of mantles worn during Biblical times. One was worn by high priests with much adornment and splendor and one of more plain quality made of white linen worn by other leaders of distinction, such as ministers, educators, and the wealthy. A mantle also reflects latitude or stature; prestige and provisions of the wearer. A mantle grants the license to act and operate. One Hebrew word for mantle "me'il" *(Strong's #4598)* is frequently applied to the "robe of the ephod". This is a tunic woven without seams and put on by being drawn over the head. In this way, the mantle covered the vital organs and intimate parts of the wearer. Another Hebrew word for mantle is "addereth" (Strong's #155) meaning a large over garment, used to describe the mantle of Elijah. While the word mantle is used 35 times in the Bible, the translation "addereth" is specifically used in reference to Elijah's cloak and glory five times. *(1 Kings 19:18-19 and 2 Kings 2:8, 13, 14)*

As they were going along and talking, behold, there appeared a chariot of fire and horses of fire which separated the two of them. And Elijah went up by a whirlwind to heaven. Elisha saw it and cried out, "My father, my father, the chariots of Israel and its horsemen!" And he saw Elijah no more. Then he took hold of his own clothes and tore them in two pieces. He also took up the mantle of Elijah that fell from him and returned and stood by the bank of the Jordan. He took the mantle of Elijah that fell from him and struck the waters and said, "Where is the Lord, the God of Elijah?"

Spriritual Understanding of a Mantle

And when he also had struck the waters, they were divided here and there; and Elisha crossed over. *(2 Kings 2:11-15 NASB)*

When Elijah was taken to heaven on a chariot of fire and a whirlwind, his mantle remained in the earth. Elijah's mantle was a natural representation of his spiritual authority. It was in placing his mantle upon the shoulders of Elisha that Elijah called him to follow. *(1 Kings 19:19)*

His mantle was left behind as a symbol of the passing of his prophetic office to Elisha. The mantle was a significant symbol that Elisha was chosen of God to continue the ministry of Prophet Elijah. It is a physical representation of the glory of God that was present in the life of Elijah. After the passing of the mantle, Elisha comes back to the Jordan River, striking the waters and dividing them as his master had done previously. Therefore, it was with this mantle that both Elijah and Elisha walked supernaturally in their anointing as prophets.

In comparison, the mantle of David was for kingship and relationship with God. The Bible tells us that David was a man after God's own heart. *(Acts 13:22)* In as much as his life is filled with accounts of failure and misconduct due to his human nature, David is also a picture of reliance on God during the tough times. Upon returning to Ziklag from battle against the Philistines, David found that his camp had been burned, the families of his soldiers taken captive, and their belongings stolen. David's fighting men wanted to stone him in anger and bitterness, but David called for the ephod and prayed to the Lord. In this moment of despair, David used the mantle of intimate relationship through prayer to receive divine strategy from on High and a guarantee of success. *(1 Samuel 30)*

David's mantle was spiritually passed to his son and heir to the throne, Solomon. Solomon understood that the only way to be a great leader was to rely on God and seek Him for all things. By his father's example, Solomon understood the power of prayer and supplication unto God. *(2 Chronicles 1:1, 7-13)*

RELEASING THE MANTLE OF PRAYER

As there was a physical mantle for Elijah and Elisha, a spiritual mantle for David and Solomon, there is a mantle available to you today. This is the mantle of prayer. There exists an untapped realm of spiritual authority through prayer and supplication unto God. The mantle of prayer will allow the Saints of God to appear before the face of God. This mantle of prayer-fueled power is evidenced by the lives of Moses, Joshua, Daniel, David, Jesus, the Apostles, and many more Biblical heroes.

Your mantle, though spiritual, will be to you a covering and a garment of unique distinction. The mantle of prayer should be worn with authority and reverence. Great Men and Women of God have impacted communities and nations with the power of prayer. By the same authority, effectiveness of purpose, and miraculous workings of God, you too can shift atmospheres and change lives by receiving the mantle of prayer.

Chapter 2

The Mantle of Prayer

Prayer is often called the Cinderella of the church. There is no human experience more common, yet confusing, more gratifying, yet frustrating, in our daily lives than prayer. There is such suspicion and doubt concerning the power of prayer that casts a veil of skepticism over religious activity. So many questions concerning the mandate of prayer permeate the minds of people regardless of ethnicity, gender, or occupation. The religious debate on the methods, purposes, and effectiveness of prayer continues today. After many years of seeking God through prayer, I can assure you that still prayer works! "The effectual fervent prayer of a righteous man availeth much." (James 5:16) In other words, the prayer of a righteous person is powerful and effective.

The terminology of prayer in the Bible is both rich and varied. Prayer means to entreat (make an earnest request), to implore (appeal, beseech), and to make a humble request before God. It also means adoration, confession, supplication, intercession, and thanksgiving. Simply put, prayer can be described as "calling upon the name of the Lord". It is worshipful supplication. Supplication is an earnest, humble request or petition such as upon bended knees. In supplication, man seeks some special grace or blessings from the Lord.

Prayer involves numerous postures and purposes. Prayer can happen while standing, sitting, kneeling, laying prostrate or even walking. Prayer times can be dedicated or spontaneous. Prayer times can include rejoicing or weeping. One can sing a song unto the Lord, as in the Book of Psalms, or lament in intercession, as Jeremiah did. Prayer can be silent, audible, in an earthly language or in heavenly tongues. Prayers can be lifted for yourself, your family, or your nation. Despite all of the ways in which one can pray and commune with God, the most important aspect is the heart with which one prays. Acceptable prayer must be sincere (Hebrews 10:22), offered with reverence and godly fear. Prayer must also be offered in the faith that God is, and is the hearer and answerer of prayer, and that He will fulfil His word, "Ask, and ye shall receive" *(Matthew 7:7,8; Mark 11:24)*

Prayer is having a conversation with God. In conversation, we not only talk; but we also listen. The full expression of prayer is one in which a petition is placed before God and an answer, direction, or word of instruction is issued in return. Our prayer requests should be given to God with opportunity for Him to respond according to His perfect will and grace in our lives. "For I know the thoughts that I think toward you, saith the Lord, thoughts of peace, and not of evil, to give you an expected end." *(Jeremiah 29:11)* In times of prayer, we ought not to lay before God a laundry list of items that need to be taken care of. Rather we speak humbly with our God and Creator, seeking His will and wisdom. Often times God will respond to our requests with some form of plan or strategy leading in the direction of the solution to our circumstance.

The prayer of agreement is a powerful prayer strategy against the devices of the enemy. Effective prayer can be accomplished individually or collectively, through prayers of agreement. "I can guarantee again that if two of you agree on anything here on earth, my Father in heaven will accept it. Where two or three have come together in my name, I am there among them." *(Matthew 18:19-20 GW)*

In the Synoptic Gospels (Matthew, Mark, and Luke) we see that Jesus went to pray alone or with certain disciples. In the garden of Gethsemane, prior to His crucifixion, Jesus took Peter, James, and John with him to pray. Finding them asleep, Jesus says, "Could you not keep watch [pray] with me one hour?" *(See Matthew 26:37-40; Mark 14:33-37; Luke 22:39-46)* Even Jesus, before the biggest assignment of His earthly ministry, took time to pray with those closest to Him. Likewise, there are people in your life whom God has elected to agree with you in prayer for the purpose of standing against the enemy and bringing God's will to pass. These prayer warriors will believe God with you and for you. Together, you can get a prayer through.

RELEASING THE MANTLE OF PRAYER

Another Biblical example of the power of the prayer of agreement is in the Book of Daniel. Daniel was a praying prophet and intercessor. Under penalty of death, Daniel and his three friends defied the king's law and continued to pray to their God. Daniel encouraged his counterparts not to give in to the idolatry of Nebuchadnezzar's edict, but instead stand firm in what was right in the eyes of God. Their fervency of prayer and dedication to the ways of God allowed Daniel to interpret dreams *(Daniel 2)*; receive divine prophetic revelation *(Daniel 9)*; and his friends, Shadrach, Meshach, and Abednego, to withstand a fiery furnace *(Daniel 3)*. Prayer is a method by which we may unlock our gifts and talents in the Lord. Prayer also allows us to withstand the tests and trials of life. Utilizing the mantle of prayer yields great results; not only for yourself, but also for those connected to you.

What makes our time in prayer even more powerful and effective is connecting it to the Word of God. We must pray and study the Word of God in order to know the will of God. Prayer is releasing the mind of God through confession of His word. *(Isaiah 55:11)* states, "So shall my word be that goeth forth out of my mouth: it shall not return unto me void, but it shall accomplish that which I please, and it shall prosper in the thing whereto I sent it."

Prayer is one of the main ways we release the will of God in our lives. This is why prayer and the Word must be combined. I heard a great Apostle once say, "The Word of God is the nail and a dedicated prayer life is the hammer that directs the nail." When we pray using the Word of God, His will is established and secured in place. Prayer and the Word of God silences the enemy. Daniel was able to pray effectively because he knew the Word of God concerning His people. *(Daniel 9:2-3)* During His time of temptation in the wilderness, Jesus was able to overcome the enemy with the Word of His Heavenly Father. Likewise, using the Scriptures while we pray assures us that we are praying God's will and speaking His promises for us. "Wherefore, be ye not unwise but understanding what the will of the Lord is." *(Ephesians 5:17)*

The Mantle of Prayer

Prayer combined with the Word of God reminds us that the thoughts of God are of peace and prosperity. God has designed a plan to bring us to an expected end. Jesus taught us that our faith is released through the words we speak. Our words prayed and spoken in faith can move mountains. *(Mark 11:23)* Prayer, undertaken during times of trial or struggle, reminds us that God has a perfect plan for us at all times. Scripture tells us, "Be anxious for nothing, but in everything by prayer and supplication with thanksgiving let your requests be made known to God. And the peace of God, which surpasses all comprehension, will guard your hearts and your minds in Christ Jesus." *(Philippians 4:6-7 NASB)* In the midst of it all we must pray with confidence and rejoicing for our expected end will cause the name of our God to be exalted. "Be still and know that I am God; I will be exalted among the heathen, I will be exalted in the earth." *(Psalm 46:10)*

Chapter 3

Touching the Mantle

I received the mantle in the wilderness. My lifelong journey of intercessory prayer began in 1988 when God gave me the spiritual assignment and mandate to stay home and pray for His people. I had no idea of the magnitude of my call or the weight of the mantle of prayer that was placed upon my life. This scepter of intercession summoned me into the presence of God, transformed me, and changed my life forever.

My whole world was literally turned upside down when I answered the call to the ministry of prayer. I did not know how expensive the price of this mantle would be or the cost of the oil. I soon found out! That "yes" to God would cost me everything. I embarked upon a time of spiritual and natural sifting, shifting, and shaking that continues to this day.

The first five years of this threshing process set me on a course into a place of separation and isolation. Separation is a necessary part and the heartbeat of the threshing process. To thresh means, "to separate grains or seeds from straw by beating the stems or husks." (freeonlinedictionary.com)

God took me into a time of cutting, stripping, purging, and cleansing on the threshing floor. He needed to separate flesh from spirit until only that which was profitable and fit for the Master's use remained. He was spiritually positioning my heart and spirit for effectual prayer. This manifest presence and hand of God formed and shaped an intercessor.

During this season of being on the Potter's wheel, there were periods of time when I could not get dressed or leave the house. I was left alone. Stuck in a holding pattern, suspended in a no name place. My prayer journal entry read "The Dark Period." There were times I could not breathe and felt I was losing my mind. The hurt and pain was so intense, I prayed for a nervous breakdown so that I might become numb and not feel it anymore.

Touching the Mantle

I just wanted it to be over. No one seemed to understand the realm I was trapped in. There could be no explanation of how I felt or the depth of this cut. God was silent, so I suffered in silence – waiting on God.

Not only was I completely isolated and separated, my family was ushered into a season of suffering and severe loss. "Stay home and pray for my people… Take care of my people and I will take care of you…," said God. Spiritually, what an honor! Then my life really began to fall apart. It was during this time of secret battles and silent wars that my family began to lose everything. After our beautiful 10-room, split-level house in the suburbs went into foreclosure, we ended up homeless; living in Room 104 of the Deer Park Motor Inn. God was still silent; but everyone else was talking about us. Friends, colleagues, and church members said we must be backslidden. I certainly needed the Lord during this test of my faith and obedience.

"And lo! a woman, having a flow of blood twelve years, coming near behind, touched the fringe of his mantle. For she kept saying within herself, – If only I touch his mantle, I shall be made well!" (Matthew 9:20-22, Rotherham) Like the woman with the issue of blood, when you're in a situation you can't get out of on your own you need to touch the mantle of the One who carries the anointing you need. The mantle represents the anointing that is able to deliver you out of your situation. I touched the mantle of my Savior, the only One who could deliver me out of this threshing place. That touch ignited the fire of the call to prayer shut up in my spirit. Thank God for that fire of confirmation and affirmation, I would need it in the years to come. Finally, my due season manifested because of the mantle and the promises of God hovering over my life. My wilderness journey to the third dimension of prayer has taken me to a place of love, intimacy, faith, and fellowship with my Lord that is priceless. It is priceless when you know how to pray.

"For our light affliction, which is but for a moment, is working for us a far more exceeding and eternal weight of glory." (2 Corinthians 4:17 NKJV)

RELEASING THE MANTLE OF PRAYER

The weight of the glory of God surely outweighs the weight of the mantle. My submission and obedience to this sovereign call has ushered my family to a place of restoration, recovery, reward, and total victory. It was worth it all to experience this realm of the glory of God!

The process of prayer never ends. *Releasing the Mantle of Prayer* has been established through years of service in prayer and intercession under the leadership of the Holy Spirit. God is now calling me as a spiritual midwife to release this mantle of prayer unto a new generation of Prayer Warriors and Intercessors that will be as Elisha to Elijah and take the miracle working power of the mantle to the next dimension of prayer.

Chapter 4

Releasing the Mantle

PThe story of Elijah and Elisha serves as a powerful example and divine pattern of the passing of the mantle. Twice the prophet released his mantle upon Elisha. The first time, to follow: "So he departed from there, and found Elisha the son of Shaphat, who was plowing with twelve yoke of oxen before him, and he was with the twelfth. Then Elijah passed by him and threw his mantle on him." *(1 Kings 19:19 NKJV)*

The second time to receive: "He took up also the mantle of Elijah that fell from him, and went back, and stood by the bank of Jordan; "And he took the mantle of Elijah that fell from him, and smote the waters, and said, Where is the Lord God of Elijah? and when he also had smitten the waters, they parted hither and thither: and Elisha went over." *(2 Kings 2:13-14)*

A true mentor imparts and releases mantles (anointing) over the lives of their spiritual children. In order to receive his inheritance, Elisha had to chase the mantle of Elijah. He had to walk through four hard places of preparation with his "father". This spiritual son had to come through Gilgal where the reproach of his former life was rolled away. Elisha learned how to overcome tests and trials at Bethel. He encountered spiritual warfare and went through a death walk at Jericho. At this place of war, Elisha completed Basic Training letting go of his desires, fears, and seeking the will of God for his life. Finally, his steadfastness, loyalty, and total commitment was confirmed as he walked with his mentor one last time to the Jordan River.

Now that Elisha passed the series of tests, at Gilgal, Bethel, Jericho and Jordan, he received the "double portion" of his father Elijah's spirit. He received the mantle, the anointing of God that was on the life of Elijah. Elijah's impartation produced a double harvest upon the life of Elisha allowing him to perform double the miracles that Elijah did. He received double for all his trouble. Elisha received beyond what he asked. And so will you!

Releasing the Mantle

Like Elisha, there are times you are broken in ways that are confusing. Nevertheless, if you submit to the process of God for your life, being obedient to the call, God will reward you in due season. He will do exceedingly, abundantly, above all you can ask or think. (Ephesians 3:20) God would never ask you to give up anything that He does not desire to replace with greater eternal results. (Matthew 19:29)

Although I was in the furnace of affliction, I was in the birthing room at the same time. During my season of suffering, the Lord birthed Restored Ministries International. Many years ago, as I cried out to God during a time of despair "I feel like I am in the Twilight Zone!!!" The Holy Spirit, lovingly whispered in my spirit, "No, you are in the Recovery Zone!" Today, The Recovery Zone Prayer Encounter is an apostolic and prophetic move of God through the power of prayer. Prayer remains the heartbeat of ministry for me. I am honored to serve every week as a spiritual midwife and apostolic parent to hundreds of intercessors and prayer warriors from around the nation convening at the altar in a supernatural place of prayer. Position yourself to be refreshed, renewed, revived, and empowered in the presence of the Most High God. As these prayer mantles are released, your life will be supernaturally transformed through the divine power of prayer. This is your spiritual "birthright" and inheritance.

The Lord took Elijah, but not his mantle. As Elijah was taken to heaven in a whirlwind, the mantle was left behind. I touched the ultimate mantle; the mantle of my Savior and now through the power of God, these mantles of prayer are released to you.

Chapter 5

Prayer to Release the Mantle of Favor

*"You will arise and have mercy on Zion;
For the time to favor her, yes, the set time has come".
Psalm 102:13 (NKJV)*

Father, in the name of Jesus, thank you for making me righteous and accepted through the Blood of Jesus Christ. I am blessed and highly favored by you. I am the object of your love and affection. Your favor surrounds me as a shield. Lord, I thank you that I have favor with you and with man every day. Let me be satisfied with your favor and filled with your blessings *(Deuteronomy 33:23)*.

I have triple favor. I have uncommon favor. I have unusual favor - favor that was, is, and will be. People are going out of their way to bless me and show me favor. I am the seed of Abraham through Jesus Christ and I receive the blessings of Abraham. Lord, in blessing, bless me, and in multiplying, multiply me as the stars in heaven and as the sand of the seashore.

I declare and confess Psalm 102:13 that this is my set time for favor. Remember me, Oh Lord with the favor that you bring unto your children and visit me with your salvation *(Psalm 106:4)*. God, I thank you that your blessings are running me down and overtaking me. I experience scandalous favor. Your favor releases me into the kingdom of the blessed *(Mark 11:10)*.

There has been a shift in my season. I have great victories supernatural turnaround, miraculous breakthroughs in the midst of great impossibilities in my life. Father, thank you, I receive extreme preferential treatment, walking in special ambassadorial privileges in your name. I am your favorite child. I am chosen by you and I am blessed *(Psalm 65:4)*.

Prayer to Release the Mantle of Favor

Your Favor releases blessings upon my storehouse and workplace. It guarantees success in everything I do *(Deuteronomy 28:8)*. I have recognition, prominence, and honor. You change decisions, policies, rulings, litigation on my behalf. Thank you for undeserved access.

I know you favor me because my enemies do not triumph over me *(Psalm 41:11)*. I win battles that I don't even have to fight because you are fighting for me. I decree and declare that my set time of favor will not be frustrated.

I am surrounded by this favor. Everywhere I walk favor follows me, leads me, and is beside me. Everywhere I go the favor of God shall go with me. It is multiplied favor and exceedingly great grace. Let your favor be upon my life as a cloud of the latter rain *(Proverbs 16:15)*. I thank you Lord that your favor arises upon me now. Favor come now. I am surrounded by this favor, supernatural favor, scandalous favor, abnormal favor, extraordinary favor, unexplainable favor, unstoppable favor, uncommon favor. I declare that favor ushers me into the presence of those who will bless me because they recognize the favor upon my life. Favor is upon every area of my life. Favor in my ministry, favor in my business, favor on my job, favor in my home, favor in my bills, favor at the bank, favor in the marketplace. Favor follows me everywhere I go.

Lord Jesus, I praise you and give you glory. I can see the place my tent enlarged. The curtains of my habitation are stretched forth, and I will spare not and will lengthen my cords and strengthen my stakes. I am breaking forth on every side, and my seed shall inherit the Gentiles and make desolate cities inhabited *(Isaiah 54:2-3)*. I declare that the Mantle of Favor is released upon my life. I decree that the anointing of favor is upon my life. I have walked into my wealthy place, in Jesus's name. Amen.

Chapter 6

Prayer to Release the Mantle of Healing and Divine Health

*"Bless the Lord, O my soul, and all that is within me,
Bless his holy name.
Bless the Lord, O my soul, and forget not all his
benefits: Who forgiveth all thine iniquities;
who healeth all thine diseases;
Who redeemeth thy life from destruction;
who crowneth thee with loving kindness
and tender mercies."
(Psalm 103:1-4)*

Father, I come to you in the volume of the Book and the power of your Word. You are the healing Balm of Gilead. Let your anointing destroy every yoke of sickness, disease, and infirmity. I command my body to come into divine alignment with your Word.

Lord Jesus, you were wounded for my transgressions, bruised for my iniquities and the chastisement of my peace was upon you and by your stripes I am already healed. Bless the fruit of my body. You are the Great Physician and your word declares: "He sent His Word, and healed them and delivered them from destruction" *(Psalm 107:20)*. Therefore, by the power of your word, I am set free from every infirmity in Jesus' name. Healing is the children's bread.

Father we know that your Word declares; "Beloved I wish above all that thou mayest prosper and be in divine health even as thy soul prospers" *(3 John 2)*. I prosper and walk in divine health even as my soul prospers. Your name releases a sound mind, restoration of divine health, and makes me whole. No sickness or plague will come near my home.

I confess that I am redeemed from the curse of the law, which included sickness and disease. My life is under a new covenant with the promise of healing, prosperity, and deliverance, in the name of Jesus. The blood of Jesus cleanses and heals me totally and completely. Behold, your name brings health and cure, peace and deliverance. I command every organ in my body to function the way God intended.

Prayer to Release the Mantle of Healing and Divine Health

I receive the Word of God, which is health to my flesh. Heal me, O Lord, and I shall be healed. Release the fire of the Most High God to burn out all sickness. Lord, you are the health of my countenance *(Psalm 43:5)*.

I take the shield of faith and quench every fiery dart of the enemy. Jesus, arise over my life with healing in your wings *(Malachi 4:2)*. Thank you Lord that you have heard my prayers, seen my tears, and released total healing to every area of my life. I rebuke every sickness that would come upon my life. I break all curses of disease and command that all hereditary spirits of sickness to come out in the name of Jesus. I will live and not die and I will proclaim the name of the Lord *(Psalm 118:17)*.

God there is nothing too hard for you. I stand against every form and fashion of sickness and disease. I cancel every assignment of mental illness; blood-borne illnesses; cancer-related illnesses; all breaks, bumps, and bruises; all parasites and viruses; all muscle disease; I rebuke tumors and cysts. I eradicate all reproductive disorders, all diseases against my organs and my skin. I command every germ to bounce off me and it shall not take root right now in the name of Jesus. I rebuke all respiratory issues right now; asthma, bronchial infection, lung disease have no place in my life. I remove all mental distress from my life: bipolar, schizophrenia, and all manic-depressive disorders have no place in my life. I rebuke nervous breakdowns and depression right now in the name of Jesus.

Your name is above every spirit of infirmity, including cancer, diabetes, high blood pressure, strokes, heart attacks, and any other spirit that would invade my life. I am healed physically. I am healed emotionally. I am totally healed from all manner of sickness and disease. I shall live a long and prosperous life as pleases the Lord my God. Neither my family nor I shall suffer premature death.

RELEASING THE MANTLE OF PRAYER

Lord, your word says:

"Is any one among you affected? Let him pray. Is any merry? Let him sing psalms? Is any sick among you? Let him call the elders of the church; and let them pray over him, anointing him with oil in the name of Jesus. And the prayer of faith shall save the sick, and the Lord shall raise him up." (James 5:13-15)

I have been made whole in the name of Jesus. Amen.

Chapter 7

Prayer to Release the Mantle of Prosperity and Financial Release

"Let them shout for joy, and be glad, that favor my righteousness cause; yea, let them say continually, Let the Lord be magnified, which hath please in prosperity of his servant"
(Psalm 35:27)

Father God, I pray for all my financial situations, in the name of Jesus. I declare that I am blessed coming in and blessed going out. Wherever the soles of my feet shall tread, prosperity belongs to me. Whatever my hands touch will prosper. I am your servant and you take pleasure in my prosperity. Lord, teach me to profit and lead me in the way I should go (Isaiah 48:17). You are Jehovah-Jireh, my provider. Lord Jesus, you became poor that through your poverty I might be rich (2 Corinthians 8:9). I thank you for the opportunity to surrender my financial dealings to you. Father, I ask that you break every generational curse and destroy every hindrance the enemy has placed on my finances, in Jesus' name. I bind the spirit of poverty, debt, covetousness, poverty mentality, inherited generational curses, wrong decisions, and disobedience.

Jehovah-Jireh, in the name of Jesus, grant unto me according to your riches in glory. I call in resources from the north, south, east, and west. I command the enemy to release all finances and resources that belong to me. I declare and decree that the wealth of the wicked is no longer laying up for me, but it is released now. Thank you, oh Lord, for bringing me into my wealthy place. Thank you for the thousand-fold increase that is coming my way.

The Lord prospers the work of my hands and I am daily loaded with benefits (Psalm 68:19). You are El-Shaddai. Therefore, I have more than enough and every empty place shall be filled to overflowing. Eternal Father, your word declares, "But thou shalt remember the Lord thy God: for it is He that giveth thee power to get wealth that He may establish His covenant which He swore unto thy fathers, as it is this day" *(Deuteronomy 8:18)*.

Prayer to Release the Mantle of Prosperity & Financial Release

I declare that I am not bound by the economy of man, but that I am under the spiritual covering of the economy of God.

I believe your prophets and I shall prosper. My gates are open continually that the wealth of the nations can come into my life. Thank you, Sovereign Lord for rebuking the devourer for my name's sake. I give and it is given to me, good measure, pressed down, shaken together, and running over *(Luke 6:38)*. Open the floodgates of heaven over my life, and I receive more than I have enough room to receive *(Malachi 3:10)*. I am blessed and I will be a blessing. Wealth and riches are in my house, oh Lord, because I fear you and delight greatly in your commandments *(Psalm 112:1-3)*. Make all grace abound towards me that I have sufficiency in all things and abound in every good work *(2 Corinthians 9:8)*. I have more coming in than I have going out and I possess riches and honor in abundance. My descendants shall forever be blessed and the spirit of poverty is cut off from my generations. I break the cycle of financial debt and bondage. I rebuke the spirit of lack and the curse of the python.

Lord, your Word declares, "but thou shalt remember us and command the blessings upon us in our storehouses, and in all that we set our hands unto; and You shall bless us in the land which You, the Lord our God, giveth us." *(Deuteronomy 28:8)* I thank you for opening the floodgates around me. I thank you for miracle money coming my way. The earth is the Lord's and the fullness thereof, the world and all who dwell therein. *(Psalm 24:1)*

Lord, let my praise activate your blessings over my life. "Let the people praise thee, O God; Let all the people praise thee. Then shall the earth yield her increase; God, our own God, shall bless us. God shall bless us," *(Psalm 67:5-6)*

I decree this day freedom and liberation from the spirit of poverty. Thank you for a new beginning of debt-free living. I declare that I will spend my days in prosperity and my years in pleasure. I am a holy millionaire, in Jesus' name. *Amen.*

Chapter
8

Prayer to Release the Mantle of Restoration and Blessing

"And it shall come to pass, if thou shalt hearken diligently unto the voice of the Lord thy God, to observe and to do all his commandments which I command thee this day, that the Lord thy God will set thee on high above all nations of the earth. And all these blessings shall come on thee, and overtake thee, if thou shalt hearken unto the voice of the Lord thy God."
(Deuteronomy 28:1-2)

Father, in the name of Jesus, we rejoice in you, thou art worthy to be praised. Thank you for being a restorer of paths to dwell in and repairer of the breach. Thank you Lord that Kairos time has kissed Chronos time and restoration is here. Lord, bless me and keep me. Make your face to shine upon me and be gracious unto me. Lord, lift up your countenance upon me and give me peace. I am chosen by God and I am blessed. Thank you for letting your presence bless my life. Let me be satisfied with your favor and filled with your blessing. Lord, I highly exalt your name for that which was held up concerning me is released now. I am blessed and will be a blessing.

Unlimited blessings shall flow like the four rivers of Eden in every area of my life. I am blessed and highly favored of God. No weapon formed against me shall be able to prosper. Every curse spoken against me is cancelled because I am truly blessed. My enemies may come against me one way, but God will cause them to flee in seven ways. Everything that the enemy has stolen is returned to me seven-fold. I am in a place of overflow and more than enough. I decree and declare that I am in The Recovery Zone.

All that I set my hands to do will flourish and prosper. I am blessed coming in and going out. The Lord has made me plenteous in goods, and I am the lender and not the borrower. I am the head and not the tail. I am above only and not beneath.

Prayer to Release the Mantle of Restoration and Blessing

Thank you, Lord Jesus, for restoring the years that the locust has eaten and the cankerworm and the caterpillar, and the palmerworm have devoured. I will eat in plenty, be satisfied, and praise the name of the Lord. This is my season of divine compensation and restitution. Thank you for turning my captivity. I am coming out of bondage and I am not coming out empty, yes, I am coming out with the spoils.

Lord, bless my latter-end more than my beginning. The place of my tent has been enlarged. The curtains of my habitation are stretched forth and I will spare not. I will lengthen my cords and strengthen my stakes. I am breaking forth on every side and my seed shall inherit the Gentiles and make desolate cities inhabited. Father, I thank you for enlarging my territory. The place that I have been in is now too small for me and I am breaking out on every side.

My gates shall be opened continually; they shall not be shut day or night. The anointing of the Mega is my portion *(Isaiah 54:2-3)*. The thief has been found and a seven-fold blessing of restoration is released upon my life.

Oh, that thou wouldest bless me indeed, enlarge my coast, and that thine hand might be with me, and that thou wouldest keep me from evil that it may not cause me pain. (1 Chronicles 4:10).

Thank you, Lord, for granting my request for your Word declares, "The blessing of the Lord, it maketh rich, and addeth no sorrow with it." *(Proverbs 10:22)* Open the windows of heaven, and pour me out a blessing that there is not room enough to receive it. Saturate me in the latter rain of your abundant riches.

You promised in your Word according to Psalm 23:5 that, "Thou preparest a table before me in the presence of mine enemies; Thou anointest my head with oil, my cup runneth over. "This is my due season. This is my time of complete restoration and suddenly blessings.

RELEASING THE MANTLE OF PRAYER

I decree and declare that the overflow of God is released upon my life, in Jesus' name. Amen.

Chapter 9

Prayer to Release the Mantle of Glory

*"O God, You are my God; early will I seek You;
my soul thirsts for You;my flesh longs for You in a dry and
thirsty land where there is no water.
So I have looked for You in the sanctuary,
to see Your power and Your glory"
(Psalm 63:1-2)*

Father in the name of Jesus, Holy is your name. I exalt thee and worship at your holy hill, for the Lord our God is holy. I thank you for access to your glory, which is the atmosphere of heaven. Invade the atmosphere of earth. Lord God, anoint me to worship you from my spirit. God is a spirit: and they that worship him must worship him in spirit and in truth. *(John 4:24)* I thank you that when the glory comes all things are possible. Lord, you are God alone and alone you are God, and I give you all the glory.

Give unto the Lord all the glory due to His name; worship the Lord in the beauty of holiness. The voice of the Lord is over the waters; the God of glory thunders; the voice of the Lord is powerful; the voice of the Lord is full of majesty. *(Psalm 29:2-4)*

Everlasting God, I invoke your presence at the very utterance of your name. Your name is above every other name. You are Wonderful, Counselor, the Mighty God, the Everlasting Father, and the Prince of Peace. Thank you for access to the glory realm, for the weight of the glory, and manifestation of your holy presence. But we all, with open face beholding as in a glass the glory of the Lord, are changed into the same image from glory to glory, even as by the Spirit of the Lord. *(2 Corinthians 3:18)*

We thank you for the glory that changes everything about our lives. Let the change happen in your glory, Father, we do not ask for your glory without giving you all of the glory. Spirit of the Living God, we declare our flesh to be silent. Increase yourself in us. Be the first and the last in us, Holy Spirit, overshadow us and endow us with your presence.

Prayer to Release the Mantle of Glory

Our Father, which art in heaven holy is your name. Anoint my words through prayer and give me legal authority both in heaven and in earth. I proclaim that you are powerful. Every valley shall be exalted and every mountain and hill brought low; the crooked places shall be made straight and rough places smooth; the glory of the Lord shall be revealed, and all flesh shall see it together; for the mouth of the Lord has spoken. *(Isaiah 40:4-5)*

God send your glory down upon our homes, churches, prisons, hospitals, and schools. God let your Glory fall fresh upon your people all across this nation and the world. Release your glory upon the youth and the minstrels, upon the choirs and the congregations. God release your glory into every circumstance and situation today, Lord. There is none like you, Lord. Your glory will turn it around.

Father, we bow down and worship thee! Holy, holy, holy, Lord God Almighty, which was, is, and is to come. Thou art worthy, O Lord, to receive glory, and honor, and power. Hallelujah to the King of Glory!

The earth is the Lord's, and the fulness thereof;
the world, and they that dwell therein.
2 For he hath founded it upon the seas,
and established it upon the floods.
3 Who shall ascend into the hill of the Lord?
or who shall stand in his holy place?
4 He that hath clean hands, and a pure heart;
who hath not lifted up his soul unto vanity,
nor sworn deceitfully.
5 He shall receive the blessing from the Lord,
and righteousness from the God of his salvation.
6 This is the generation of them that seek him,
that seek thy face, O Jacob. Selah.
7 Lift up your heads, O ye gates;

RELEASING THE MANTLE OF PRAYER

and be ye lift up, ye everlasting doors;
and the King of glory shall come in.
8 Who is this King of glory?
The Lord strong and mighty,
the Lord mighty in battle.
9 Lift up your heads, O ye gates;
even lift them up, ye everlasting doors;
and the King of glory shall come in.
10 Who is this King of glory?
The Lord of hosts,
he is the King of glory. Selah.
(Psalm 24)

Lord, show me Thy Glory! Amen.

Chapter 10

The Power of Prayer

In sharing these powerful prayers and miraculous testimonies from The Recovery Zone Prayer Encounter, it is my heart's desire that you will be encouraged, edified, and empowered to continue your personal journey of prayer. As you read the following testimonies of supernatural signs, miracles, and wonders happening in the lives of praying people just like you, know that God is no respecter of persons, what He does for one He can do for all. *(Acts 10:34-35)* God can and will answer your prayers according to your faith. *(Matthew 9:29)* Pray in faith, with believing and conviction that the name of God is a strong tower and the righteous shall run therein and be safe. *(Proverbs 18:10)*

**Testimony of Pastor Sandra Gainey,
Mullins, SC**

On the morning of March 11, 2015, I had the opportunity to speak to Apostle Banks after our time of prayer concluded. She shared with me that as the Word was going forth she could see a dark cloud moving from over Mullins, SC. Apostle Banks began to prophesy that not only did she see the dark cloud moving, but also she saw my ministry bursting out of the seams! Apostle Banks stated that she saw God moving for us like never before with no more delays, no more hindrances, etc.

Praise be to God, her words were true! Since that morning, doors have come open for the ministry just as she said they would! For three years, our ministry had been using a community recreational center and my home for church services. But thanks be to God, a building came forth!! Not only did God provide a permanent location for us, but also our monthly expenses are just what we asked God for. God, doing exceedingly and abundantly, gave us a building that is double the size we expected!! We asked that our rent be due in the middle of the month and our landlord has honored our request!! God has favored us to find everything we need to convert the building into a sanctuary for Him at an affordable price. The paint, pulpit, offering table, chairs, etc. God has granted us divine favor with every merchant and company we have communicated with. God has even granted favor to my personal ministry with an increase in requests for speaking engagements.

The Power of Prayer

**Testimony of Sister Cynthia Myers,
Georgetown, SC**

It was in the overflow of our Wednesday Prayer Encounter that you were praying for another person. You prayed for her eyes as she had been suffering from partial blindness. I felt the Holy Ghost instruct me to lay hands on my own eyes. In obedience to the prompting, I laid hands on myself and received the words you were praying over the other Woman of God.

I immediately began to feel a warm sensation going through my eyes. When you finished praying I removed my hands and I looked across the room where my grandchild's "ABC chart" hangs on the wall. I realized that, I could recognize the letters, colors, and numbers on the chart! I was so excited because even that morning before prayer I was unable to distinguish objects from that distance. I had been diagnosed with glaucoma over 10 years ago. My doctors told me that whatever sight I lost as a result of the glaucoma would not return. Since that morning some of my sight has been returned. I continue to rejoice and believe God for total Healing and Restoration.

**Testimony of Missionary Rosemary Baker-Fuller,
Orlando, FL**

I want to give thanks to God for all what he has done. My oldest brother, James O. Baker, was on crack cocaine for 30 years. He has served 5 years in prison for gun and drug charges. He was caught again with an illegal gun. He had five strikes against him. In Alabama, that is automatically 25 years to life in prison. It was two years before he was given another court date. He was still looking at the possibility of 25 to life.

I had been getting on Apostle Banks' 5am prayer call every Wednesday morning and lifting my brother and his situation in prayer. I also purchased her Prayer Packs Things Happen at Midnight, It's Just a Smoke Screen, and The Threat is Over. I listened to them repeatedly. Prayer is real!

RELEASING THE MANTLE OF PRAYER

The day we went to court, the public defender told me that he believed James was really only looking at the possibility of three years of jail time. I replied that for all my brother had been through he was not going anywhere. I told him it was only a smoke screen and the threat is over.

When the court session began, the judge was giving everyone time to serve. James's turn in front of the judge was different. First, the judge told him to relax there was no need to be scared. Then, the judge showed the courtroom a before and after picture of James saying that James looked even better now than in his after picture. The judge even requested to speak privately with my husband and me.

By the end of this unusual encounter, the judge did not give James 25 to life or three years in jail. He told my brother that he was giving him three years of probation so he could go enjoy his children and grandchildren. From 25 to life to three years of probation! But God!!

As if that were not enough of a blessing from God, my brother completed two years of his probation and he is now a free man!

Testimony of Marie Goodall
Bridgeport, CT

I have been suffering with chronic migraines for the past 44 years. This particular day I had a migraine while I was on my way to work. When I got to work everyone knew I had a migraine as it was very noticeable. My face says it all. I got home at approximately 3:30 pm and rushed to my room where I began to pray and ask God to deliver me from such pain. I repeated continuously, "Not again Lord. Not again."

Whenever there is an attack of migraines, it can last for 3 to 4 days. I have taken up to twelve pills hoping they would help, but there is no relief. The migraine has to take its course. This particular night, I went to bed with my face covered as I am extremely sensitive to light during this time. When suddenly I remembered Apostle Banks had mailed me a prayer pack, "The Threat is Over."

The Power of Prayer

It was delivered to someone else's address, however, the lady brought it to my house.

I said to myself, I am going to play it. But then I thought, no because I am also sensitive to sounds and this will make my head hurt more. Finally, I said to myself, you know what I don't care. I am going to listen to it and turn the volume down. The CD played all night. I got up the following morning saying "the Giant is Dead!" I repeated it aloud saying, the giant of migraine you are dead! At this point, the headache was minor and I got dressed and went to work. I got to work at 7:00am and realized that the headache was gone. All day I wanted to run and shout "the Giant is dead!" But, I had to control myself because I was at work. Thank God for His healing power.

Testimony of Sister Jannette Celestine
Sheldon, South Carolina/Queens, New York

On December 21, 2014 I received a call that my son Bernard Celestine, age 36, had a massive stroke. At the time, I was in South Carolina and Bernard was in New York. When I arrived to the hospital, the doctors showed me a scan of his head and the damage that had been done. I said, Doctor, you see my son's head, but I see God. Bernard laid in ICU for over a week. The doctors began to release him from the respirator to see if he could breathe on his own. After an hour he was breathing on his own. A half hour later he was still breathing on his own. The doctors yelled, "Look at God!!! It's a MIRACLE. But if he lives he would be a vegetable." Then they said Bernard could be in a wheelchair the rest of his life. I said, with the God I serve he will walk and talk.

During this time, I joined The Recovery Zone Prayer Encounter. Throughout this entire time I was decreeing and declaring that Bernard's right side would be restored and the blood circulation would be restored. In one room the patient died, in another room the patient died. I believed God that Bernard would live and not die. The devil said, "your son is next". I jumped up and anointed the door even though I had already anointed the room. I demanded death to flee in Jesus Name.

RELEASING THE MANTLE OF PRAYER

The next day Bernard was being wheeled out of that room and into a step down area. He was talking and eating everything he asked for. On April 17, 2015 Apostle Banks personally visited Bernard at the St. Johnland Rehabilitation Center. She prayed for him and released miracles of healing and deliverance according to the Word and power of God.

On June 16, my 71st birthday, my son, whom the doctors said would be a vegetable and would be unable to walk or talk, called me on the phone and sang Happy Birthday in its entirety! He sang all the way through to how old are you now, staying in tune the whole time.

All glory to God, on July 13, 2015 Bernard was released from the rehab center and is now at home!

I thank God for the prayers of the saints and anointed prayer warriors like Apostle Banks.

**Testimony of Cessane Sapp,
Orlando, FL**

Glory be to the name of our Lord. I have worked for the Federal Government for over 16 years. In September 2009, I filed an EEOC case against my employer for discrimination. It was a long battle filled with a tremendous amount of stress, anxiety, depression, investigations, interrogations, and isolation. In March 2014, I received a court order that my case would be heard during the second week of December. As I began to prepare my case, I felt this overwhelming weight that seemed to get heavier. I just wanted to say forget about it and throw in the towel. The enemy continued to harass and torment me. I was weak in my spirit and nobody around me realize I was bleeding out. I cried out to the Lord, what should I do, should I just let this case go or should I continue on?

The following week I received my answer from God through this powerful Prayer Pack "It's Just a Smoke Screen" by Apostle Elise Banks. This word encouraged, strengthened, and empowered me to pursue. To get up and go past every obstacle in the name of the Lord.

The Power of Prayer

I listened to that CD everywhere I went - in my car, on my job and at home until I had it downloaded in my spirit. The more I listened to the CD the stronger I became. I replenished my arsenal, put on my war clothes and pursued in the name of the Lord. I called The Recovery Zone Prayer Encounter and told Apostle Banks how the Prayer Packs continued to encourage and strengthen me. Apostle Banks prayed for me and the EEOC case. Several months passed. One day while on the Prayer Encounter, Apostle said somebody needs to check their bank account because a settlement has been deposited. After the prayer call, I checked my account and there was settlement money in my account!

Apostle Banks and The Recovery Zone Prayer Encounter have changed my life. I truly recommend the Prayer Packs to everyone. I call them Weapons of Mass Destruction against any warfare you may be experiencing in your life.

The Recovery Zone Prayer Encounter is where you can encounter the Lord.

Testimony of Apostle Lemuel Smith
Wilmington, DE

For the last ten years I have been going back and forward with the court systems. There has been a lot of witchcraft and demonic devices being used against me in the midst of my situation. Using my weapons of spiritual warfare I prayed, fasted, and continually sought God for answers. It seemed like nothing was happening fast enough.

Well in the ninth year, we were informed that the Court messed up - they began to double dipping on my payments. Because we were on top of our end of the situation, they were not allowed to enforce this on me. My wife and I began to pray together and the Lord spoke concerning this matter in the tenth year of this ongoing situation. It was during the second year of the double payments that the Lord turned the whole situation around in a matter of ten days. A ten-year problem, two years of overcharges, during one of those two years my paperwork was held up in cyber space…

RELEASING THE MANTLE OF PRAYER

But God turned it around, it was turned around in less than ten days after He spoke a word of confirmation to my wife and me on The Recovery Zone Prayer Encounter.

Now, I have been released from under the marine spirit attack that was holding up my financial release!
Praise the Lord!

Testimony of Ronalda Sedeno
Lansdowne, PA

The Recovery Zone Prayer Encounter is a place where you can truly encounter the Lord. Times of deep prayer and prophetic intercession may activate a vision within us. Answers to prayer or words of confirmation sometimes come through these visions. Think it not strange that your responses from the Lord come in the form of a visual picture as opposed to an audible sound.

I share with you this testimony of prophetic vision that turned out to be a word of confirmation from the Lord; not for me, but for Apostle Banks herself.

VISION 4.22.15
I was present with you (Apostle Banks) while you were doing a live TV interview on CNN. I was watching from the behind the cameras. I understood that it was the morning show. The anchor had been interviewing you on an unknown topic and during the interview you went into a prophetic flow. The anointing that was on you overflowed to her and the anchor began to declare the names of people who were being loosed from bondage, sin, strongholds, and other hindering spirits.

I had a feeling of concern in my stomach about how viewers would respond to the change in their morning program. I thought that many viewers would be in an uproar about having prayer and apostolic flow going across their screens so freely. But my initial thought, that is my natural mind, was wrong.

The Power of Prayer

Holy Spirit showed me a view of the anchor's desk. If you have ever seen the anchor's desk they have tablets or computer screens in front of them. The anchor was actually on CNN's Social Media sites and there were people all across the country commenting with prayer requests and the names of their family members who needed to be loosed from bondage. People all across the nation were being swept into the flow of God and declaring in unity that they were coming out of bondage.

Prayer was being televised on secular television - unscheduled.

I shared this vision with Apostle Banks via email as the Holy Spirit impressed upon me that it was important for her to see the words and read them, not just hear them by phone. In response to my email, Apostle Banks forwarded me a request she had received to appear on a television program and discuss the mandate of prayer. As the Lord would have it, she received the appearance request and my email containing confirmation within two hours of each other! The vision that I received during the 5am Prayer Encounter was an answer to an invitation that did not come to her until that afternoon.

The Spirit of the Lord is always working and active. Able to confirm, warn, redirect, and encourage according to our need. As Apostle Banks says, prayer changes things and prayer changes the people who pray. I am grateful unto God for connecting me to The Recovery Zone Prayer Encounter in order that I may Encounter His Glory on a weekly basis!

Chapter 11

An Encounter with Glory

"Now the Lord is the Spirit; and where the Spirit of the Lord is, there is liberty. But we all, with unveiled face, beholding as in a mirror the glory of the Lord, are being transformed into the same image from glory to glory, just as by the Spirit of the Lord."
2 Corinthians 3:17-18 (NJKV)

Prayer is a spiritual experience and where the Spirit of God is there is freedom. Each time you worship God in prayer, His presence liberates you and you will develop a deeper level of communication and relationship with Him. Prayer just doesn't change things – Prayer changes everything and Prayer changes those who pray.

The threshing floor is the place of total surrender to God in prayer and intercession. God will lead you through transforming stages of process until you step into His glory. He does not just want you to see His glory, but that God gets all the glory out of your life.

The glory realm is the third dimension of prayer. Prayer in the third dimension releases a deeper desire within you to please God and stay in His presence. When you enter the glory of this realm in prayer your flesh becomes silent, your spirit ascends to a supernatural place of communication and communion with Almighty God. Being in the presence of God, being quiet before Him will make you totally surrender to the will and purpose of God for your life, be filled in your spirit.

"But the Lord is in His holy temple. Let all the earth keep silence before Him." (Habakkuk 2:20, NKJV)

Glory is the revelation and manifestation of the divine presence of God. It indicates a witness of the favor and grace of God. Glory includes honor, prestige, power and blessings. The presence of God brings increase in every area of our lives and glory is an automatic deposit of the grace and anointing of God.

An Encounter with Glory

As the air that we breathe is the atmosphere of earth, glory is the atmosphere of heaven. When the glory comes down, heaven's atmosphere comes down to us. When we encounter the third dimension, the glory realm of prayer, heaven is manifesting on earth.

The essence of prayer, intercession and worship should permeate the atmosphere around you. This is the sweet aroma of prayer. The divine threshing process of God begins at the outer court to the most holy place of prayer all the way into His divine presence behind the veil. This is the most intimate dimension of prayer.

Prayer is My Passion
My Rhythm
My Heartbeat
My Ministry
My Mandate
My Mission
My Mantle
My Life

The highest call in the Kingdom of God is prayer. God is calling you to the altar of Prayer. He is mantling you for the greater. The mantle on my life covers you. Move into the glory realm and all things become possible. Come behind the veil into the third dimension of prayer and the divine presence of Almighty God. This is the place of intimacy and fellowship, where you will receive the mantle of prayer and experience an encounter with glory.

"In the year that king Uzziah died I saw also the Lord sitting upon a throne, high and lifted up, and his train filled the temple.

Above it stood the seraphims: each one had six wings; with twain he covered his face, and with twain he covered his feet, and with twain he did fly.
And one cried unto another, and said, Holy, holy, holy, is the Lord of hosts: the whole earth is full of his glory."
Isaiah 6:1-3

The mantle is yours!

About the Author

Dr. **Elise Banks** is the Founder and Visionary of **Restored Ministries International, Incorporated**, an itinerant evangelistic ministry for prayer, restoration, and deliverance. The mandate on her life is to the call of a kingdom revivalist, whose assignment is to encourage, empower, and restore the hurting, downtrodden, and outcast. Her mission is to reach all who are spiritually bankrupt with a message of victory through Jesus Christ.

She has received the call, commission, and power to do the will and the work of the Lord. She is divinely clothed with a prophetic mantle and radical anointing. This woman of God is loyal and steadfast in her commitment to ministry. She serves as an intercessory prayer warrior and prayer counselor, culminating in the establishment of The Recovery Zone Prayer services, conferences and prayer lines. She has served as a Bible Institute professor and is a certified chaplain. She travels extensively ministering as a revivalist, conference speaker and workshop facilitator, boldly preaching and teaching the Word of God.

Fulfilling her divine authority, appointment, and affirmation as an Apostle of the Lord's Church she provides apostolic oversight and spiritual covering for numerous churches and ministries and is a mighty and yielded instrument in the hands of an Almighty God. She is blessed with the spirit of compassion and love for all people, as a result of her own personal years of suffering and severe loss.

Restored Ministries International, Incorporated, is under the spiritual covering of **Dr. Banks's** Apostolic Father Archbishop Alfred A. Owens, Jr., Pastor of Greater Mount Calvary Holy Church, Washington, D.C., and the International Presiding Prelate of Mount Calvary Holy Church of America, Incorporated.

A native of Charleston, South Carolina, **Dr. Banks** earned her Master of Theology Degree, Master of Religious Education Degree, and Doctor of Sacred Theology Degree from United Christian College.

She received the Doctor of Divinity Degree and Doctor of Christian Philosophy from the Eagle Bible Institute and Seminary.

Dr. Banks is the proud mother of two daughters, Doria and Keesha, and the grandmother of one grandson, Kamron. This unique vessel comes boldly declaring her love for her Lord, Jesus Christ, with whom all things are possible and through whom all things are restored.

Releasing the Mantle of Prayer

Prayer Strategy

Prayer List

DATE   REQUEST   SCRIPTURE
                                        PROMISE

DATE	REQUEST	SCRIPTURE PROMISE

DATE	REQUEST	SCRIPTURE PROMISE

DATE	REQUEST	SCRIPTURE PROMISE

Notes

The Recovery Zone Prayer Encounter

Every Wednesday Morning @ 5am EST
Dial: 1-712-432-0075 / Access Code: 430698#

Contact:
Restored Ministries International
P.O. Box 886
Lindenhurst, NY 11757
1-877-804-7274
info@restoredintl.org
www.restoredintl.org

Restored Ministries International
@DrEliseBanks

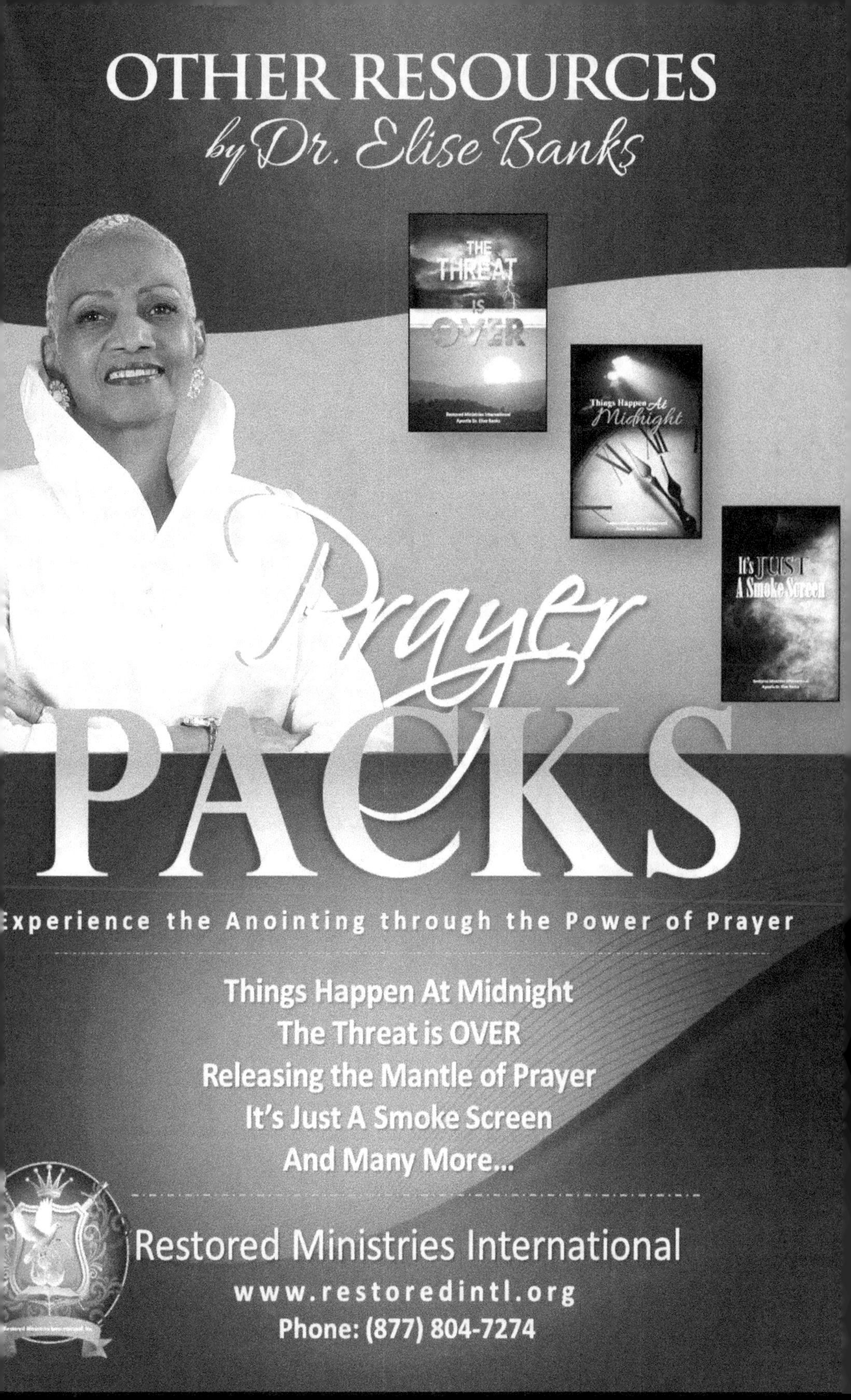

OTHER RESOURCES
by Dr. Elise Banks

Prayer PACKS

Experience the Anointing through the Power of Prayer

Things Happen At Midnight
The Threat is OVER
Releasing the Mantle of Prayer
It's Just A Smoke Screen
And Many More...

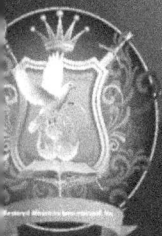

Restored Ministries International
www.restoredintl.org
Phone: (877) 804-7274

www.ingramcontent.com/pod-product-compliance
Lightning Source LLC
Chambersburg PA
CBHW072103290426
44110CB00014B/1808